The Best of Mary Maxim®

MW01091681

Baby Afghans

2

6

9

19

22

24

27

LEISURE ARTS, INC. • Maumelle, Arkansas

Sugar Spun Blanket

Caron — 3 Skeins

SHOPPING LIST

Yarn (DK/Sportweight) LIGHT 3

[3.5 ounces, 295 yards
(100 grams, 270 meters) per ball]:
☐ 3 balls self-striping yarn

Crochet Hook

☐ Size G-6 (4.00 mm)
or size needed for gauge

SIZE INFORMATION

Size: 36" diameter (91.5 cm)

GAUGE INFORMATION

Rnds 1-5 = 5.25" [13 cm] measured
over pattern, using suggested hook
or any size hook which will give the
correct stitch gauge.

— STITCH GUIDE —

FPdc - Front Post Double Crochet:
Yo, insert hook from front to back
to front around post of indicated
st, yo and pull up a loop, [yo and
draw through 2 loops on hook]
twice.

dc2tog: [Yo, insert hook in next
st, yo and draw up a loop, yo and
draw through 2 loops on hook]
twice, yo and draw through all 3
loops on hook.

dc3tog: [Yo, insert hook in st
indicated, yo and draw up a loop,
yo and draw through 2 loops
on hook] 3 times, yo and draw
through all 4 loops on hook.

dc4tog: [Yo, insert hook in st
indicated, yo and draw up a loop,
yo and draw through 2 loops
on hook] 4 times, yo and draw
through all 5 loops on hook.

INSTRUCTIONS

Ch 7, join with sl st to form a ring.

Rnd 1: Ch 3 (counts as first dc
throughout), 2 dc in ring, [ch 2,
3 dc in ring] 5 times, ch 2, join with
sl st in top of beg dc.

Rnd 2: Ch 3, dc in same st, dc in
next dc, 2 dc in next dc,
*ch 2, 2 dc in next dc, dc in next dc,
2 dc in next dc; rep from * around,
ch 2, join with sl st in top of beg
dc. (30 dc, 6 ch-2 loops).

Rnd 3: Ch 3, dc in same st, dc in
each of next 3 dc, 2 dc in next dc,
*ch 3, 2 dc in next dc, dc in each of
next 3 dc, 2 dc in next dc; rep from
* around, ch 3, join. (42 dc, 6 ch-3
loops)

Rnd 4: Ch 3, dc in same st, dc in
each of next 5 dc, 2 dc in next dc,
*ch 2, dc in next sp, ch 2, 2 dc in
next dc, dc in each of next 5 dc,
2 dc in next dc; rep from * around,
ch 2, dc in next sp, ch 2, join.
(60 dc, 12 ch-2 loops)

Rnd 5: Ch 3, dc in same st, dc in
each of next 7 dc, 2 dc in next dc,
*ch 2, FPdc in next dc, ch 2, 2 dc in
next dc, dc in each of next 7 dc,
2 dc in next dc; rep from * around,
ch 2, FPdc around next dc, ch 2,
join.

Rnd 6: Ch 3, dc in same st, dc in each of next 9 dc, 2 dc in next dc, *ch 3, FPdc around next FPdc, ch 3, 2 dc in next dc, dc in each of next 9 dc, 2 dc in next dc; rep from * around, ch 3, FPdc around next FPdc, ch 3, join.

Rnd 7: As Rnd 6, but working 11 dc instead of 9 dc.

Rnd 8: Ch 3, dc in same st, dc in each of next 13 dc, 2 dc in next dc, *ch 4, FPdc around next FPdc, ch 4, 2 dc in next dc, dc in each of next 13 dc, 2 dc in next dc; rep from * around, ch 4, FPdc around next FPdc, ch 4, join.

Rnd 9: Ch 3, dc in each of next 16 dc, *ch 2, FPdc around next FPdc [ch 2, FPdc around same FPdc] twice and working each FPdc below each one by turning your work sideways, ch 2**, dc in each of next 17 dc; rep from * around ending last rep at **, join.

Rnd 10: Ch 3, dc in each of next 16 dc, *ch 3, FPdc around next FPdc, [ch 2, FPdc around next FPdc] twice, ch 3**, dc in each of next 17 dc; rep from * around ending last rep at **, join.

Rnd 11: Ch 3, dc in each of next 16 dc, *ch 3, [FPdc around next FPdc, ch 2] twice, FPdc around next FPdc, ch 3**, dc in each of next 17 dc; rep from * around ending last rep at **, join with sl st in top of beg dc.

Rnd 12: Ch 2, dc in next dc - (counts as first dc2tog), dc in each of next 13 dc, *dc2tog, ch 3, 3 dc in next FPdc, ch 3, FPdc around next FPdc, ch 3, 3 dc in next FPdc, ch 3**, dc2tog, dc in each of next 13 dc; rep from * around ending last rep at **, join with sl st in top of first dc2tog.

Rnd 13: Work first dc2tog (as in Rnd 12), dc in each of next 11 dc, *dc2tog, ch 4, (2 dc in next dc, dc in next dc, 2 dc in next dc,

ch 4), FPdc around next FPdc, ch 4, rep from (to) once**, dc2tog, dc in each of next 11 dc; rep from * around ending last rep at **, join.

Rnd 14: Work first dc2tog (as in Rnd 12), dc in each of next 9 dc, *dc2tog, ch 2, dc in next ch-sp, ch 2, dc in each of next 5 dc, ch 4, FPdc around next FPdc, ch 4, dc in each of next 5 dc, ch 2, dc in next ch-sp, ch 2**, dc2tog, dc in each of next 9 dc; rep from * around ending last rep at **, join.

Rnd 15: Work first dc2tog (as in Rnd 12), dc in each of next 7 dc, *dc2tog, ch 3, FPdc around next dc, ch 3, dc2tog, dc in next dc, dc2tog, ch 4, 5 dc in next FPdc, ch 4, dc2tog, dc in next dc, dc2tog, ch 3, FPdc around next dc, ch 3**, dc2tog, dc in each of next 7 dc; rep from * around ending last rep at **, join.

Rnd 16: Work first dc2tog (as in Rnd 12), dc in each of next 5 dc, *dc2tog, [ch 3, dc in next ch-sp] twice, ch 3, dc3tog, ch 3, 2 dc in next dc, dc in each of next 3 dc,

2 dc in next dc, ch 3, dc3tog, [ch 3, dc in next ch-sp] twice, ch 3**, dc2tog, dc in each of next 5 dc; rep from * around ending last rep at **, join.

Rnd 17: Work first dc2tog (as in Rnd 12), dc in each of next 3 dc, *dc2tog, ch 3, [dc in next ch-sp, ch 3] 4 times, dc2tog, dc in each of next 3 dc, dc2tog, ch 3, [dc in next ch-sp, ch 3] 4 times**, dc2tog, dc in each of next 3 dc; rep from * around ending last rep at **, join.

Rnd 18: Work first dc2tog (as in Rnd 12), dc in next dc, *dc2tog, [ch 3, dc in next ch-sp] 5 times, ch 3, dc2tog, dc in next dc, dc2tog, [ch 3, dc in next ch-sp] 5 times, ch 3**, dc2tog, dc in next dc; rep from * around ending last rep at **, join.

Rnd 19: Ch 3, dc in next dc (counts as first dc2tog), *[ch 3, dc in next ch-sp] 6 times, ch 3**, dc2tog; rep from * around ending last rep at **, join with sl st in top of dc2tog.

Rnd 20: Sl st in next ch-sp, ch 3, 2 dc in same sp, *3 dc in next ch-sp; rep from * around, join with sl st in top of beg dc. (252 dc)

Rnd 21: Ch 3, dc in each of next 2 dc, ch 3, skip next dc, *dc in each of next 3 dc, ch 3, skip next dc; rep from * around, join. (63 ch sps)

Rnd 22: Sl st to next ch-sp, (ch 3, dc, ch 2, sc) in first ch-3 sp, ch 2, *(2 dc, ch 2, sc) in next ch-3 sp, ch 2; rep from * around, join.

Rnd 23: Ch 3, dc in same st as join, dc in next dc, ch 3, *2 dc in next dc, dc in next dc, ch 3; rep from * around, join with sl st in top of beg ch-3. (63 ch-sps)

Rnd 24: Sl st to next ch-sp, (ch 3, 2 dc) in first ch-3 sp, ch 2, skip next dc, sc in next dc, ch 2, *3 dc in next ch-3 sp, ch 2, skip next dc, sc in next dc, ch 2; rep from * around, join with sl st in top of beg dc. (189 dc)

Rnd 25: Sl st to first ch-2 sp, (ch 3, 2 dc) in first ch-2 sp, ch 2, sc in center dc of next 3-dc group, ch 2, *3 dc in next ch-2 sp, ch 2, sc in center dc of next 3-dc group,

ch 2; rep from * around, join with sl st in top of beg dc.

Rnd 26: Ch 3, dc in each of next 2 dc, ch 3, *dc in each of next 3 dc, ch 3; rep from * around, join with sl st in top of beg dc. (189 dc)

Rnd 27: Sc in next dc, ch 2, *3 dc in next ch-3 sp, ch 2, sc in center dc of next 3-dc group, ch 2; rep from * around, join with sl st in first sc.

Rnd 28: Sl st to first dc, ch 3, dc in each of next 2 dc, ch 4, *dc in each of next 3 dc, ch 4; rep from * around, join with sl st in top of beg dc.

Rnd 29: Ch 3, dc in same st as joining and in each of next 2 dc, 4 dc in next ch-4 sp, *dc in each of next 3 dc, 4 dc in next ch-4 sp; rep from * around, join. (442) dc.

Rnd 30: *Ch 5, skip next dc, dc4tog over next 4 sts, *ch 4, sl st in 4th ch from hook* - **Picot made,** ch 5, skip next dc, sc in next dc; rep from * around, ending last rep with sl st in base of beg ch-5. Fasten off.

Baby Diamonds Blanket

Caron A - 3 skeins
" B - 1 "

INTERMEDIATE

SIZE INFORMATION

Size: 38 x 44" (96.5 x 111.5 cm)

GAUGE INFORMATION

17 sc and 16 rows to 4" [10 cm] measured over single crochet using suggested hook or any size hook which will give the correct stitch gauge.

— STITCH GUIDE —

PC - Popcorn: All worked in next stitch. Yarn over hook, insert hook in stitch indicated, draw up loop, [yarn over hook, insert hook in same stitch] 4 times, yarn over hook and draw through all 11 loops on hook.

After working PC stitch, make sure to push PC to the right side of work.

sc2tog: [Insert hook in next st and draw up a loop] twice, yarn over hook and draw through all 3 loops on hook. Decrease made.

INSTRUCTIONS

Panel I: Using Color A, ch 3.

Row 1: (right side) Work 3 sc in 3rd ch from hook, ch 1, turn. (3 sts)

Row 2: Sc in each st across, ch 1, turn.

Row 3: Work 2 sc in first st (inc made), sc in next st, 2 sc in last st, ch 1, turn. (5 sts)

Row 4: Sc in each of first 2 sts, PC in next st, sc in each of next 2 sts, ch 1, turn.

Row 5: Work 2 sc in first st, sc in each of next 3 sts, 2 sc in last st, ch 1, turn. (7 sts)

Row 6: Sc in each of first 2 sts, PC in next st, sc in next st, PC in next st, sc in each of last 2 sts, ch 1, turn.

Row 7: Work 2 sc in first st, sc in each of next 5 sts, 2 sc in last st, ch 1, turn. (9 sts)

Row 8: Sc in each of first 2 sts, PC in next st, sc in each of next 3 sts, PC in next st, sc in each of last 2 sts, ch 1, turn.

Row 9: Work 2 sc in first st, sc in each of next 7 sts, 2 sc in last st, ch 1, turn. (11 sts)

Continue in this manner, inc on every odd row, and PC on every even row, having 2 sts before PC at the beg of the row and 2 sts after PC at the end of the row, until there are 17 sts, and ending on an inc row (right side).

Row 16: Sc in each of first 2 sts, PC in next st, sc in each of next 5 sts, PC in next st, sc in each of next 5 sts, PC in next st, sc in each of last 2 sts.

Row 17: Sc2tog over first 2 sts, sc in each of next 13 sts, sc2tog over last 2 sts, ch 1, turn. (15 sts)

Row 18: Sc in each of first 2 sts, PC in next st, sc in each of next 9 sts, PC in next st, sc in each of next 2 sts, ch 1, turn.

Row 19: Sc2tog, sc in each of next 11 sts, sc2tog, ch 1, turn. (13 sts)

Row 20: Sc in each of first 2 sts, PC in next st, sc in each of next 7 sts, PC in next st, sc in each of last 2 sts, ch 1, turn.

Row 21: Sc2tog, sc in each of next 9 sts, sc2tog, ch 1, turn. (11 sts)

Row 22: Sc in each of first 2 sts, PC in next st, sc in each of next 5 sts, PC in next st, sc in each of last 2 sts, ch 1, turn.

Row 23: Sc2tog, sc in each of next 7 sts, sc2tog, ch 1, turn. (9 sts)

Row 24: Sc in each of next 2 sts, PC in next st, sc in each of next 3 sts, PC in next st, sc in each of last 2 sts, ch 1, turn.

Row 25: Sc2tog, sc in each of next 5 sts, sc2tog, ch 1, turn. (7 sts)

Row 26: Sc in each of first 2 sts, PC in next st, sc in next st, PC in next st, sc in each of last 2 sts, ch 1, turn.

Row 27: Sc2tog, sc in each of next 3 sts, sc2tog, ch 1, turn. (5 sts)

Row 28: Sc in each of first 2 sts, PC in next st, sc in each of last 2 sts, ch 1, turn.

Row 29: Sc2tog, sc in next st, sc2tog, ch 1, turn. (3 sts)

Repeat Rows 2 - 29, 5 times more.

Row 170: Sc in each of next 3 sts, ch 1, turn.

Row 171: [Insert in next st and draw up a loop] 3 times, yo and draw through all 4 loops on hook. Draw loop through rem st to fasten off.

Make 6 more panels using Color A.

Panel II: (Make 3 using Color B and 3 using Color C).
Work as for Panel I, using the correct color, but repeating Rows 2 - 29, 4 times more.

To Assemble: Join Panels together with single crochet using B for panel B, and C for Panel C, in the following sequence:
A, B, A, C, A, B, A, C, A, B, A, C, A.
When joining, pin panels together with widest part to narrowest part. See diagram below.

EDGING: Using Color A, join to any corner with a sl st, *ch 4, sl st in 4th ch from hook - **Picot made,** sc in next st on blanket; rep from * around, working approximately 12 Picots along each side of diamond on top and bottom of work and approximately 17 Picots along each diamond at the sides, around to beg Picot, join with a sl st in base of beg Picot.
Fasten off. Sew all loose ends in.

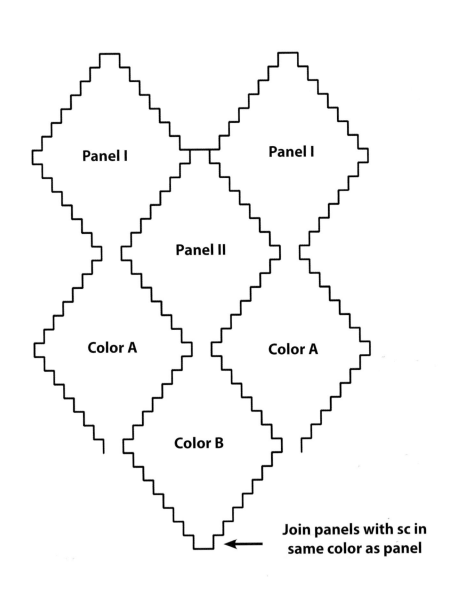

Panel I

Panel I

Panel II

Color A

Color A

Color B

Join panels with sc in same color as panel

Bears on My Blanket

INTERMEDIATE

Caron 6/balls - 3 skein (handwritten)

SIZE INFORMATION

Size: 31 x 44" (78.5 x 111.5 cm)

GAUGE INFORMATION

19 sts and 21 rows to 4" [10 cm] measured over single crochet using suggested hook or any size hook which will give the correct stitch gauge.

Bears: 8 sts and 9 rows to 2" [5 cm] measured over single crochet using suggested hook or any size hook which will give the correct stitch gauge or tension.

— STITCH GUIDE —

sc2tog: [Insert hook in next st and draw up a loop] twice, yo and draw through all 3 loops on hook

Note: In order to simplify afghan, a diagram of afghan will be used. Each bear is shown separate from the diagram in order to better describe bear pieces and sewing order.

INSTRUCTIONS

Basic Afghan: The basic afghan consists of windows and borders. There will be 9 windows, 6 side borders, 2 middle borders, 2 short (top/bottom) borders, and 2 long (left/right) borders.

Afghan Diagram

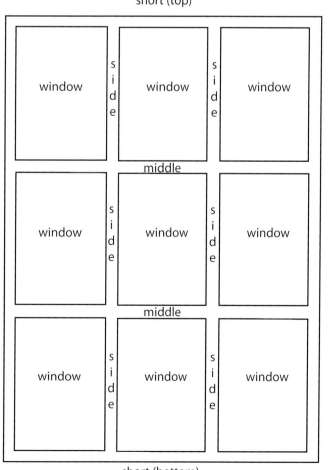

Window: (make 9)

Using MC, ch 36.

Row 1: Sc in 2nd ch from hook and in each ch to end, ch 1, turn - 35 sc.

Rows 2-58: Sc in each sc across, ch 1, turn. Fasten off.

Window side: (make 6)

Note: Be sure gauge is correct and sides fit exactly to windows. You can adjust number of sts if necessary.

Using Color 1, ch 53.

Row 1: Sc in 2nd ch from hook and in each ch to end, ch 1, turn - 52 sc.

Rows 2-8: Sc in each sc across, ch 1, turn. Fasten off.

Window middle: (make 2)

Using Color 1, ch 122.

Row 1: Sc in 2nd ch from hook and in each ch to end, ch 1, turn - 121 sc.

Rows 2-8: Sc in each sc across, ch 1, turn. Fasten off.

Following diagram, sew all pieces tog as illustrated.

Short Borders: (worked across top and bottom edges of afghan) With right side facing, using Color 1, work 121 sc evenly across one short edge; working 35 sc across each window and 8 sc across each side, ch 1, turn.

Row 1: Sc in each sc across, ch 1, turn -121 sc.

Rows 2-4: Sc in each sc across, ch 1, turn. Fasten off.

Repeat for other short edge.

Long Borders: With right side facing, using Color 1, work 198 sc evenly along one long edge of afghan; working 58 sc along each window, 8 sc along each middle section and 4 sc across each short end, ch 1, turn.

Row 1: Sc in each sc across, ch 1, turn -198 sc.

Rows 2-4: Sc in each sc across, ch 1, turn. Fasten off.

Repeat for other side of afghan.

Heart Border: Worked across each short edge and each side edge with corner hearts made separately and sewn in place.

Note: The border along each short edge will have 9 hearts (with 3 sc between each heart) and each long edge will have 15 hearts (with 2 sc between each heart).

Short Heart Border: Using Color 1, with right side of afghan facing, join in top corner and work 129 sc evenly across, ch 1, turn.

Row 2: Sc in each sc across, ch 1, turn - 129 sts.

Row 3: Sc in each of first 3 sts, *sc in each of next 5 sts, ch 2, skip next st, sc in each of next 8 sts; rep from * to end, ch 1 turn.

Row 4: Sc in each of first 3 sts, *sc in each of next 4 sts, ch 2, skip next st, sc in ch-2 space, ch 2, skip next st, sc in each of next 7 sts; rep from * to end, ch 1, turn.

Row 5: Sc in each of first 3 sts, *sc in each of next 3 sts, ch 2, skip next st, sc in ch-2 space, sc in next st, sc in ch-2 space, ch 2, skip next st, sc in each of next 6 sts; rep from * to end, ch 1, turn.

Row 6: Sc in each of first 3 sts, *sc in each of next 2 sts, ch 2, skip next st, sc in ch-2 space, sc in each of next 3 sts, sc in ch-2 space, ch 2, skip next st, sc in each of next 5 sts; rep from * to end, ch 1, turn.

Row 7: Sc in each of first 3 sts, *sc in next st, ch 2, skip next st, sc in ch-2 space, sc in each of next 5 sts, sc in ch-2 space, ch 2, skip next st, sc in each of next 4 sts; rep from * to end, ch 1, turn.

Row 8: Sc in each of first 3 sts, *ch 2, skip next st, sc in ch-2 space, sc in each of next 7 sts, sc in ch-2 space, ch 2, skip next st, sc in each of next 3 sts; rep from * to end, ch 1, turn.

Row 9: Sc in each of first 3 sts, *ch 1, skip ch-2 space, sc in each of next 9 sts, ch 1, skip ch-2 space, sc in each of next 3 sts; rep from * to end, ch 1, turn.

Row 10: Sl st in first 3 sts, *sl st in ch-1 space, 2 dc in next st, tr in

each of next 2 sts, 2 dc in next st, sl st in next st, 2 dc in next st, tr in each of next 2 sts, 2 dc in next st, sl st in ch-1 space, sl st in each of next 3 sts; rep from * to end. Fasten off.

Repeat on other short end.

Long Heart Border: Using Color 1, with right side of afghan facing, join in corner and work 198 sc evenly across, ch 1, turn.

Row 2: Sc in each sc across, ch 1, turn -198 sc.

Row 3: Sc in each of first 3 sts, *sc in each of next 5 sts, ch 2, skip next st, sc in each of next 7 sts; rep from * to end, ch 1 turn.

Row 4: Sc in each of first 2 sts, *sc in each of next 4 sts, ch 2, skip next st, sc in ch-2 space, ch 2, skip next st, sc in each of next 6 sts; rep from * to last st, sc in last st, ch 1, turn.

Row 5: Sc in each of first 3 sts, *sc in each of next 3 sts, ch 2, skip next st, sc in ch-2 space, sc in next st, sc in ch-2 space, ch 2, skip next st, sc in each of next 5 sts; rep from * to end, ch 1, turn.

Row 6: Sc in each of first 2 sts, *sc in each of next 2 sts, ch 2, skip next st, sc in ch-2 space, sc in each of next 3 sts, sc in ch-2 space, ch 2, skip next st, sc in each of next 4 sts; rep from * to last st, sc in last st, ch 1, turn.

Row 7: Sc in each of first 3 sts, *sc in next st, ch 2, skip next st, sc in ch-2 space, sc in each of next 5 sts, sc in ch-2 space, ch 2, skip next st, sc in each of next 3 sts; rep from * to end, ch 1, turn.

Row 8: Sc in each of first 2 sts, *ch 2, skip next st, sc in ch-2 space, sc in each of next 7 sts, sc in ch-2 space, ch 2, skip next st, sc in each of next 2 sts; rep from * to last st, sc in last st, ch 1, turn.

Row 9: Sc in each of first 3 sts, *ch 1, skip ch-2 space, sc in each of next 9 sts, ch 1, skip ch-2 space, sc in each of next 2 sts; rep from * to end, ch 1, turn.

Row 10: Sl st in first 2 sts, *sl st in ch-1 space, 2 dc in next st, tr in each of next 2 sts, 2 dc in next st, sl st in next st, 2 dc in next st, tr in

each of next 2 sts, 2 dc in next st, sl st in ch-1 space, sl st in each of next 2 sts; rep from * to last st, sl st in last st. Fasten off.

Repeat along other long edge.

Corner Heart: (make 4)

Using Color 1, ch 2.

Row 1: Work 3 sc in 2nd ch from hook, ch 1, turn - 3 sc.

Row 2: Work 2 sc in first st, sc in next st, 2 sc in last st, ch 1, turn - 5 sc.

Row 3: Sc in each of first 2 sts, ch 2, skip next st, sc in each of next 2 sts, ch 1, turn.

Row 4: Work 2 sc in first st, ch 2, skip next st, sc in ch-2 space, ch 2, skip next st, 2 sc in last st, ch 1, turn - 5 sc and 2 ch-2 sp.

Row 5: Work 2 sc in first st, ch 2, skip next st, sc in ch-2 space, sc in next st, sc in ch-2 space, ch 2, skip next st, 2 sc in last st, ch 1, turn - 7 sc and 2 ch-2 sp.

Row 6: Work 2 sc in first st, ch 2, skip next st, sc in ch-2 space, sc in each of next 3 sts, sc in ch-2 space, ch 2, skip next st, 2 sc in last st, ch 1, turn - 9 sc and 2 ch-2 sp.

Row 7: Work 2 sc in first st, ch 2, skip next st, sc in ch-2 space, sc in each of next 5 sts, sc in ch-2 space, ch 2, skip next st, 2 sc in last st, ch 1, turn - 11 sc and 2 ch-2 sp.

Row 8: Work 2 sc in first st, ch 2, skip next st, sc in ch-2 space, sc in each of next 7 sts, sc in ch-2 space, ch 2, skip next st, 2 sc in last st, ch 1, turn - 13 sc and 2 ch-2 sp.

Row 9: Sc in first st, ch 1, skip ch-2 space, sc in each of next 9 sts, ch 1, skip next st, sc in last st, ch 1, turn - 11 sc.

Row 10: Sl st in first st, sl st in ch-1 space, 2 dc in next st, tr in each of next 2 sts, 2 dc in next st, sl st in next st, 2 dc in next st, tr in each of next 2 sts, 2 dc in next st, sl st in ch-1 space, sl st in last st. Fasten off.

Sew a heart into each corner of heart border.

STAR BEAR star and **HEART BEAR** heart must be sewn on prior to attaching left arm paws. By doing this paws can be positioned over heart and star.

Basic Bear Head: (make 5)

Using Color 6, ch 11.

Row 1: Work 2 sc in 2nd ch from hook, sc in each of next 8 ch, 2 sc in last ch, ch 1, turn - 12 sc.

Row 2: Work 2 sc in first st, sc in each of next 10 sts, 2 sc in last st, ch 1, turn - 14 sc.

Rows 3-5: Work as Row 2 - 20 sc after Row 5.

Rows 6-12: Sc in each sc across, ch 1, turn.

Row 13: Sc2tog over first 2 sts, sc in each sc to last 2 sts, sc2tog, ch 1, turn - 18 sc.

Rows 14-17: Work as Row 13 - 10 sc after Row 17. Fasten off.

Basic Bear Body: (make 3)

Using Color 6, ch 11.

Rows 1-5: Work Rows 1-5 as given for Basic Bear Head.

Rows 6-17: Sc in each sc across, ch 1, turn.

Rows 18-22: Work Rows 13-17 as given for Basic Bear Head. Fasten off.

Basic Bear Muzzle: (make 4)

Using Color 6, ch 7.

Row 1: Work 2 sc in 2nd ch from hook, sc in each ch across to last ch, 2 sc in last ch, ch 1, turn - 8 sc.

Row 2: Work 2 sc in first st, sc in each of next 6 sts, 2 sc in last st, ch 1, turn - 10 sc.

Row 3: Work as Row 2 - 12 sc.

Rows 4-6: Sc in each sc across, ch 1, turn.

Row 7: Sc2tog over first two sts, sc in each of next 8 sts, sc2tog, ch 1, turn - 10 sc.

Row 8: Work as Row 7 - 8 sc. Fasten off.

Basic Bear Ears: (make 5 pairs)

Using Color 6, ch 5.

Row 1: Work 2 sc in 2nd ch from hook, sc in each of next 2 ch, 2 sc in last ch, ch 1, turn - 6 sc.

Rows 2-4: Sc in each sc across, ch 1, turn.

Row 5: Sc2tog over first two sts, sc in each of next 2 sts, sc2tog, ch 1, turn - 4 sc.

Row 6: Work 15 sts around edge of ear as follows: sc in same st, sc in each of next 3 sts up side of ear, 2 sc in corner st, sc in each of next 2 sts across top of ear, 2 sc in corner st, sc in each of next 4 sts down side of ear, and sc in first stitch of last row. Fasten off.

Basic Bear Tail: (make 3)
Using Color 6, ch 4.

Row 1: Work 2 sc in 2nd ch from hook, sc in next ch, 2 sc in last ch, ch 1, turn - 5 sc.

Rows 2-3: Sc in each sc across, ch 1, turn.

Row 4: Sc2tog, sc in next st, sc2tog, ch 1, turn -3 sc. Fasten off.

Basic Bear Arm: (make 5)
Using Color 6, ch 7.

Row 1: Work 2 sc in 2nd ch from hook, sc in each of next 4 ch, 2 sc in last ch, ch 1, turn - 8 sc.

Row 2: Work 2 sc in first st, sc in each of next 6 sts, 2 sc in last st, ch 1, turn - 10 sc.

Rows 3-10: Sc in each sc across, ch 1, turn.

Row 11: Sc2tog, sc in each of next 7 sts, 2 sc in last st, ch 1, turn - 10 sc.

Rows 12-14: Sc in each sc across, ch 1, turn.

Row 15: Sc2tog, sc in each of next 7 sts, 2 sc in last st, ch 1, turn - 10 sc.

Rows 16-18: Sc in each sc across, ch 1, turn.

Row 19: Sc2tog, sc in each of next 7 sts, 2 sc in last st, ch 1, turn - 10 sc.

Rows 20-24: Sc in each sc across, ch 1, turn. Fasten off.

Basic Bear Leg: (make 2 pairs)
Using Color 6, ch 7.

Row 1: Work 2 sc in 2nd ch from hook, sc in each of next 4 ch, 2 sc in last ch, ch 1, turn - 8 sc.

Row 2: Work 2 sc in first st, sc in each of next 6 sts, 2 sc in last st, ch 1, turn - 10 sc.

Rows 3-10: Sc in each sc across, ch 1, turn.

Row 11: Sc2tog, sc in each of next 7 sts, 2 sc in last st, ch 1, turn - 10 sc.

Row 12: Sc in each sc across, ch 1, turn.

Rows 13-16: Repeat last two rows - 10 sc.

Rows 17-18: Sc in each sc across, ch 1, turn.

Row 19: [Sc2tog] twice, sc in each of next 5 sts, 2 sc in last st, ch 1, turn - 9 sc.

Row 20: Sc in each sc across, ch 1, turn.

Row 21: [Sc2tog] twice, sc in each of next 4 sts, 2 sc in last st, ch 1, turn - 8 sc.

Row 22: Sc in each sc across, ch 1, turn.

Row 23: Sc2tog, sc in each of next 5 sts, 2 sc in last st, ch 1, turn - 8 sc.

Row 24: Sc in each st across. Fasten off.

To Assemble: Using black yarn, embroider all face detail as shown for each bear. Following Diagrams and sewing order as listed for each bear, pin pieces to afghan to get correct placement, then sew each piece in place. On all bears facing forward, attach ears just inside last row worked around ear.

Balloon Bear: (sew pieces in place as shown)

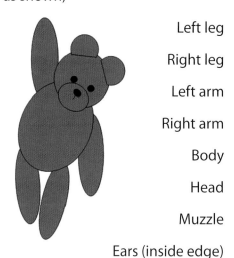

Left leg
Right leg
Left arm
Right arm
Body
Head
Muzzle
Ears (inside edge)

Reaching for Star Bear: (sew pieces in place as shown)

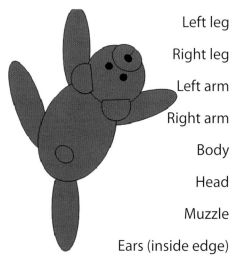

Left leg
Right leg
Left arm
Right arm
Body
Head
Muzzle
Ears (inside edge)
Tail

Heart Bear:

Heart Bear Paw: (make 1)

Using Color 6, ch 7.

Row 1: Work 2 sc in 2nd ch from hook, sc in each of next 4 ch, 2 sc in last st, ch 1, turn - 8 sc.

Row 2: Work 2 sc in first st, sc in each of next 6 sts, 2 sc in last st, ch 1, turn - 10 sc.

Rows 3-5: Sc in each sc across, ch 1, turn.

Row 6: Sc2tog, sc in each of next 6 sts, sc2tog, ch 1, turn - 8 sc.

Row 7: Sc2tog, sc in each of next 4 sts, sc2tog - 6 sc.

Fasten off.

(sew pieces in place as shown)

Left arm
Right paw
Head
Muzzle
Ears (inside edge)

Sleeping Bear:

Sleeping Bear Body: (make 1)

Using Color 6, ch 8.

Row 1: Work 2 sc in 2nd ch from hook, sc in each of next 5 ch, 2 sc in last st, ch 1, turn - 9 sc.

Row 2: Work 2 sc in first st, sc in each of next 7 sts, 2 sc in last st, ch 1, turn - 11 sc.

Row 3: Work 2 sc in first st, sc in each st to end, ch 1, turn - 12 sc.

Row 4: Sc to last st, 2 sc in last st, ch 1, turn - 13 sc.

Row 5: Work 2 sc in first st, sc in each st to end, ch 1, turn - 14 sc.

Row 6: Sc in each sc across, 2 sc in last st, ch 1, turn - 15 sc.

Rows 7-10: Sc in each st across, ch 1, turn.

Fasten off.

Sleeping Bear Neck: (make 1)

Using Color 6, ch 16.

Row 1: Sc in 2nd ch from hook and in each ch to end, ch 1, turn - 15 sc.

Row 2: Sc in each st across, ch 1, turn - 15 sc.

Row 3: Sc in each st to last 2 sts, sc2tog, ch 1, turn - 14 sc.

Row 4: Sc2tog, sc in each st across, ch 1, turn - 13 sc.

Row 5: Sc in each st to last 2 sts, sc2tog, ch 1, turn - 12 sc.

Row 6: Sc2tog, sc in each st to end, ch 1, turn - 11 sc.

Row 7: Sc in each sc across to last 2 sts, sc2tog, ch 1, turn - 10 sc. Fasten off.

(sew pieces in place as shown)

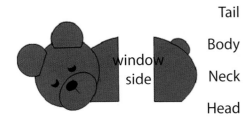

Tail
Body
window side
Neck
Head
Muzzle
Ears

Back End Bear:

Back End Bear Arms: (make 2)

Using Color 6, ch 7.

Row 1: Work 2 sc in 2nd ch from hook, sc in of next 4 ch, 2 sc in last st, ch 1, turn - 8 sc.

Row 2: Work 2 sc in first st, sc in each of next 6 sts, 2 sc in last st, ch 1, turn - 10 sc.

Rows 3-10: Sc in each sc to end, ch 1, turn.

Row 11: Sc2tog over first two sts, sc in each sc to last 2 sts, sc2tog, ch 1, turn - 8 sc.

Row 12: Work as Row 11 - 6 sc. Fasten off.

Back End Bear Legs: (make 2)

Using Color 6, ch 7.

Rows 1 and 2: Work as given for Arms above.

Rows 3-7: Sc in each sc to end, ch 1, turn.

Rows 8 and 9: Work Rows 11 and 12 as given for arms. Fasten off.

(sew pieces in place as shown)

Left arm
Right arm
Left leg
Right leg
Body
Ears (overcast)
Head
Tail

Balloon:

Using Color 3, ch 13.

Row 1: Work 2 sc in 2nd ch from hook, sc in each of next 10 ch, 2 sc in last ch, ch 1, turn - 14 sc.

Row 2: Work 2 sc in first st, sc in each of next 12 sts, 2 sc in last st, ch 1, turn - 16.

Rows 3-7: Work as Row 2 - ending with 26 sc.

Rows 8-25: Sc in each sc across, ch 1, turn.

Row 26: Sc2tog over first two sts, sc in each sc to last 2 sts, sc2tog, ch 1, turn - 24 sc.

Rows 27-37: Repeat last row 11 more times -ending with 2 sc.

Row 38: Work 2 sc in first st, 2 sc in last st, ch 1, turn - 4 sc.

Row 39: Work 2 sc in first st, sc in each of next 2 sts, 2 sc in last st - 6 sc.

Fasten off.

Balloon string:

Using Color 3, ch 115.

Fasten off.

To Assemble: Pin balloon into position, then sew in place. Sew string in place (as shown in color picture), using a straight stitch in center of ch loops. String can be positioned into the bear's paw by weaving string in and out of two sc holes on paw.

Star: (MUST be attached before Star Bear's left paw)

Center of Star: Using Color 4, ch 7.

Row 1: Sc in 2nd ch from hook and in each ch to end, ch 1, turn - 6 sc.

Row 2: Work 2 sc in first st, sc in each st across, 2 sc in last st, ch 1, turn - 8 sc.

Row 3: Sc in each st to end, ch 1, turn.

Rows 4-7: Repeat last two rows twice - ending with 12 sc.

Row 8: Sc2tog over first two sts, sc in each st to last 2 sts, sc2tog, ch 1, turn - 10 sc.

Row 9: Sc in each sc across, ch 1, turn.

Rows 10-13: Repeat last two rows twice - ending with 6 sc.

Rows 14-15: Sc in each sc across, ch 1, turn.

Row 16: Sc2tog, sc in each sc to last 2 sts, sc2tog, ch 1, turn - 4 sc.

Rows 17-18: Sc in each sc to end, ch 1, turn.

Row 19: [Sc2tog] twice, ch 1, turn - 2 sc.

Rows 20-21: Sc in each sc across, ch 1, turn.

Row 22: Sc2tog. Fasten off.

Star Points:

Using Color 4.

Row 1: Work 6 sc on any side, ch 1, turn.

Rows 2-3: Sc in each sc across, ch 1, turn.

Row 4: Sc2tog, sc in each of next 2 sts, sc2tog, ch 1, turn - 4 sc.

Rows 5-6: Sc in each sc across, ch 1, turn.

Row 7: [Sc2tog] twice, ch 1, turn - 2 sc.

Rows 8-9: Sc in each sc across, ch 1, turn.

Row 10: Sc2tog. Fasten off.

Repeat 4 times for each side of center of star that is not worked.

Star Tails: (make 3)

Using Color 4, ch 40. Fasten off.

To Assemble: Pin center of star in position and sew into place. Pin star tails in position and sew in place using a straight stitch in center of ch loops. To get tails around window side, immediately

before window side pull tail down through a sc hole and then pull tail back up through a sc hole on opposite side of window side.

Heart: (MUST be attached before Heart Bear's left arm paw). Top of heart will be worked in two separate pieces, then worked tog.

First Half: Using Color 5, ch 6.

Row 1: Work 2 sc in 2nd ch from hook, sc in each ch across to last ch, 2 sc in last ch, ch 1, turn - 7 sc.

Row 2: Work 2 sc in first st, sc in each st to last st, 2 sc in last st, ch 1, turn - 9 sc.

Rows 3-4: Repeat last row twice - ending with 13 sc. Fasten off.

Second Half: Using Color 5, ch 6. Repeat 4 rows given for First Half, DO NOT fasten off after last row, ch 1, turn.

Row 5: Sc in each of first 13 sts, sc in 13 sts of Second Half, ch 1, turn - 26 sc.

Rows 6-14: Sc in each sc across, ch 1, turn - 26 sc.

Rows 15-27: Sc2tog, sc in each st to last 2 sts, sc2tog, ch 1, turn - ending with one sc.
Fasten off.
Sew heart in place as shown in color picture.

Footprints: (make 5 paw pads and 20 toes - 4 for each paw pad)

Paw Pad: Using Color 2, ch 6.

Row 1: Work 2 sc in 2nd ch from hook, sc in each ch across to last ch, 2 sc in last ch, ch 1, turn - 7 sc.

Rows 2-4: Work 2 sc in first st, sc in each st to last st, 2 sc in last st, ch 1, turn - ending with 13 sc.

Rows 5-9: Sc in each st to end, ch 1, turn.

Rows 10-13: Sc2tog, sc in each sc to last 2 sts, sc2tog, ch 1, turn - ending with 5 sc.
Fasten off.

Toe: Using Color 2, ch 3.

Row 1: Work 2 sc in 2nd ch from hook, 2 sc in last ch, ch 1, turn - 4 sc.

Row 2: Sc in each st to end, ch 1, turn.

Row 3: [Sc2tog] twice - 2 sc.
Fasten off.
Sew pieces in place as shown in color picture.

Z's: (make 3 different sizes)

Large Z: Using Color 3, ch 40. Fasten off.

Medium Z: Using Color 3, ch 30. Fasten off.

Small Z: Using Color 3, ch 20. Fasten off.

To Assemble: Pin Z's in position and sew in place using a straight stitch in center of ch loops.

Placement Diagram

Tiny Bubbles Blanket

EASY

SHOPPING LIST

Yarn (Worsted Weight)
[6 ounces, 315 yards
(170 grams, 288 meters) per skein]:

- ☐ Main Color   White - 3 skeins
- ☐ Color A   Yellow - 1 skein
- ☐ Color B   Pink - 1 skein
- ☐ Color C   Orchid - 1 skein
- ☐ Color D   Blue - 1 skein
- ☐ Color E   Green - 1 skein

Crochet Hook

- ☐ Size E-4 (3.50 mm)
  or size needed for gauge

SIZE INFORMATION

Size: 36 x 38" (91.5 x 96.5 cm)

GAUGE INFORMATION

One motif measures approximately 2" [5 cm] across at widest point, using suggested hook or any size hook which will give the correct gauge.

─── STITCH GUIDE ───

Beg Cl - Beginning Cluster; Ch 2, [yo, insert hook in ring and draw up a loop, yo and draw through 2 loops on hook] twice, yo and draw through all 3 loops on hook.

Cl - Cluster; [Yo, insert hook in ring and draw up a loop, yo and draw through 2 loops on hook] 3 times, yo and draw through all 4 loops on hook.

Pattern Notes:

1. Motifs are worked with right side facing throughout.

2. The first motif is worked and finished off. Then the next motifs are worked, one at a time, and joined to previous motifs while working Round 2 (joining round).

3. Make and join by first joining motifs into one row of 18 motifs. Then make and join the next row of motifs, one at a time. If you make and join motifs in this order, each will only need to be joined to one edge of one or two previous motifs.

4. Refer to assembly diagram for placement of white and colored motifs. Each colored motif may be color of your choice.

5. A total of 388 motifs are worked, 136 white motifs, and 252 colored motifs (50 or 51 of each color).

6. Please note, color photo shows wrong sides of motifs used as right side of afghan.

Motifs are reversible, but always use the same side for right side when joining.

───────────

INSTRUCTIONS

First Motif (make one using any contrast color)

Ch 6, join with sl st in first ch to form ring.

Rnd 1: (right side) Beg Cl in ring, ch 3, [Cl in ring, ch 3] 5 times, join with sl st in top of Beg Cl. (6 clusters)

Rnd 2: [(Sc, ch 3, sc) in next ch-3 sp, ch 2] 6 times, join with sl st in first sc. Fasten off.

Next Motif (See diagram; #2 is Main color, etc)

Using MC, ch 6, join with sl st in first ch to form ring.

Rnd 1: Work as Rnd 1 of First Motif. Determine placement for motif (refer to assembly diagram) and work appropriate Rnd 2 (joining rnd). When joining current motif to previous motif(s), hold with wrong sides together, and with sides to be joined aligned.

Rnd 2: (Joining one side to one previous motif)

(Sc, ch 3, sc) in next ch-3 sp of current motif, ch 2, [sc in next ch-3 sp of current motif, ch 1, sc in corresponding ch-3 sp of previous motif, ch 1, sc in same ch-3 sp of current motif, ch 2] twice, [(sc, ch 3, sc) in next ch-3 sp of current motif, ch 2] 3 times; join with sl st in first sc. Fasten off.

Rnd 2: (Joining two sides to two previous motifs)

(Sc, ch 3, sc) in next ch-3 sp of current motif, ch 2, [sc in next ch-3 sp of current motif, ch 1, sc in corresponding ch-3 sp of previous motif, ch 1, sc in same ch-3 sp of current motif, ch 2] twice for rows beg with white motifs or 3 times for rows beg with color motifs,

[(sc, ch 3, sc) in next ch-3 sp of current motif, ch 2] twice; join with sl st in first sc. Fasten off.

Border: With right side facing, join MC with sl st in any ch-3 sp of a corner motif.

Rnd 1: Ch 1, work sc around entire outside edge as follows: work 3 sc in each outer corner ch-3 sp (motif point), 2 sc in each ch-2 sp (on side of motifs), and 2 sc in each inner corner ch-3 sp (the ch-3 sps on either side of a join between motifs); join with sl st in first sc. Fasten off.

Placement Diagram

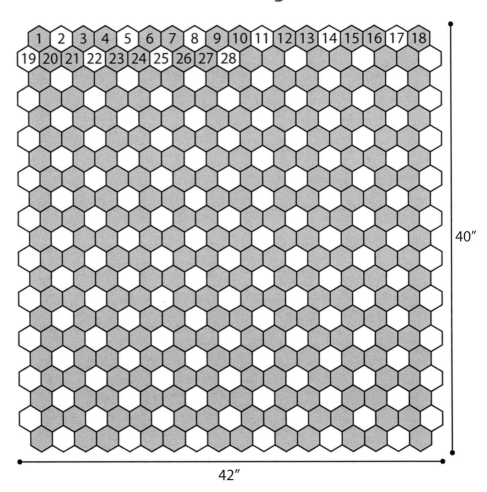

40"

42"

◯ White motif

⬡ Color motif, color of your choice

Note: Numbers in hexagons indicate recommended order of joining. If you join in this order, each motif needs to be joined to one side of at most two motifs.

Rnd 2: With right side facing, join Color A with sl st in any sc, ch 1, sc in each sc around, working 3 sc in center sc of each motif point, and skipping 2 sc at each inner corner; join with sl st in first sc. Fasten off.

Rnd 3: With right side facing, join Color B with sl st in any sc, repeat Rnd 2. Fasten off.

Rnd 4: With right side facing, join Color C with sl st in any sc, repeat Rnd 2. Fasten off.

Rnd 5: With right side facing, join Color D with sl st in any sc, repeat Rnd 2. Fasten off.

Rnd 6: With right side facing, join Color E with sl st in any sc, repeat Rnd 2. Fasten off.

Rnd 7: With right side facing, join MC with sl st in any sc, repeat Rnd 2. Fasten off.

Duckies Blanket

SHOPPING LIST

Yarn (Worsted Weight) **4** MEDIUM

[3.5 ounces, 180 yards
(100 grams, 165 meters) per ball]:

☐ Yellow - 7 balls

Crochet Hook

☐ Size H-8 (5.00 mm)
or size needed for gauge

SIZE INFORMATION

Size: 38.5 x 43.5" (97.5 x 110.5 cm)

GAUGE INFORMATION

12 dc and 6 rows to 3" [7.5 cm],

measured over double crochet using

suggested hook or any size hook

which will give the correct gauge.

INSTRUCTIONS

Ch 156.

Now following Graph, rep 3 times

across, working as follows:

Row 1: (right side) Dc in 4th ch

from hook and in each ch to end,

turn - 154 dc (including beg ch-3).

Row 2: Ch 3, dc in each of next 3

dc, *[ch 2, skip next 2 dc, dc in next

dc] 15 times, [dc in each of next 3

dc] twice; rep from * twice more,

but ending last rep with dc in each

of last 3 dc, turn.

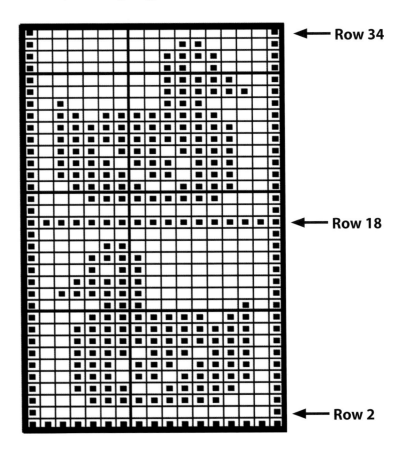

← Row 34

← Row 18

← Row 2

STITCH GUIDE

☐ = Mesh - ch 2, skip 2 sts, dc in next st

▣ = Block - dc in each of next 3 sts
beg Block worked at the beg of each row is ch 3,
dc in each of next 3 dc.
Beg ch 3 is used and counted as a st.

Row 3: Ch 3, dc in each of next 3 dc (beg Block), *[ch 2, skip next 2 ch, dc in next dc] 3 times (3 mesh), [dc in each of next 2 ch, dc in next dc] 9 times (9 blocks), [ch 2, skip next 2 ch, dc in next dc] 3 times (3 mesh), [dc in each of next 3 dc] twice (2 blocks); rep from * twice more, but ending last rep with dc in each of last 3 dc (one block), turn.

Now continue to work graph as shown until 34 rows have been completed.

Repeat Rows 1-34 once, then Rows 1-18 once more - 87 rows in all. Break yarn and fasten off.

Peaceful Pastels Afghan

■■□□ EASY

Color or Verigated = 8 skeins (handwritten)

SHOPPING LIST

Yarn (DK/Sportweight) LIGHT 3

[5 ounces, 388 yards (140 grams, 355 meters) per skein]:

- ☐ Color 1 Green - 2 skeins
- ☐ Color 2 Blue - 2 skeins
- ☐ Color 3 Purple - 2 skeins
- ☐ Color 4 Pink - 1 skein
- ☐ Color 5 Peach - 1 skein
- ☐ Color 6 Yellow - 1 skein
- ☐ Color 7 White - 1 skein

Crochet Hook

- ☐ Size K-10.5 (7.00 mm) or size needed for gauge

SIZE INFORMATION

Size: 50" (127 cm) diameter

GAUGE INFORMATION

5 rounds to 4" [10 cm] measured from center out to a point using suggested hook or any size hook which will give the correct stitch gauge.

— STITCH GUIDE —

Shell - Work (2 dc, ch 2, 2 dc) in space or stitch indicated.

Beg Shell - Work (ch 3, dc, ch 2, 2 dc) in space or stitch indicated.

Small Shell - Work (dc, ch 2, dc) in space or stitch indicated.

Note: Afghan is worked using 2 strands of yarn throughout. The afghan is worked in rounds.

INSTRUCTIONS

Using 2 strands of Color 7, ch 4, join with sl st to form ring.

Rnd 1: Ch 3, work 11 dc in ring, join with sl st in top of beg ch-3 - 12 dc.

Rnd 2: Ch 3, dc in same sp, 2 dc in each st around, join in top of beg ch-3 - 24 dc.

Rnd 3: Ch 3, *skip next st, (dc, ch 2, dc) in next st; rep from * around, ending with dc in base of beg ch-3, ch 2, sl st in top of beg ch-3 - 12 Small Shells.

Rnd 4: Break one strand of Color 7, join one strand Color 6 and sl st in ch-2 sp, work Beg Shell in same sp, *Shell in next ch-2 sp; rep from * around, join in top of beg ch-3 - 12 Shells.

Rnd 5: Sl st in next st, ch 3, *Shell in next ch-2 sp, dc in next dc, skip next 2 dc, dc in next st; rep from * around, join in top of beg ch-3.

Rnd 6: Break Color 7 strand, join second strand of Color 6 and sl st in next st, ch 3, dc in next st, *Shell in next ch-2 sp, dc in each of next 2 dc, skip next 2 sts, dc in each of next 2 dc; rep from * around, ending with skip 2 sts, join in top of beg ch-3.

Rnd 7: Sl st in next st, ch 3, dc in each of next 2 sts, *Small Shell in next ch-2 sp, dc in each of next 3 sts, skip 2 sts, dc in each of next 3 sts; rep from * ending with skip 2 sts, join in top of beg ch-3.

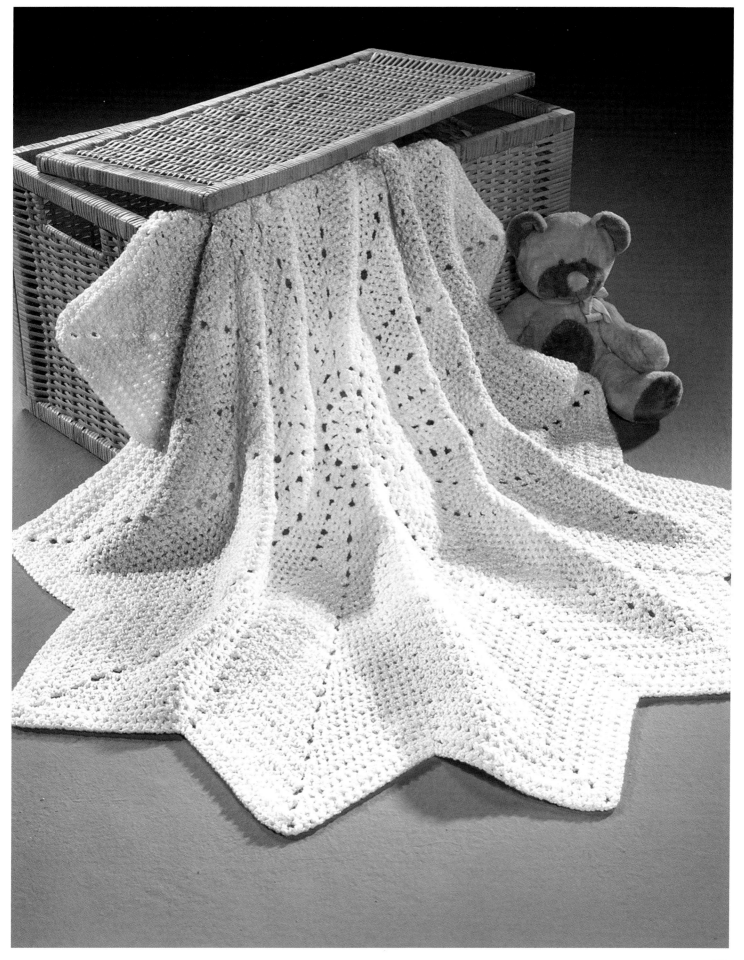

Rnd 8: Break one strand of Color 6, join one strand Color 5 and sl st in next st, ch 3, dc in each of next 2 sts, *Shell in ch-2 sp, dc in each of next 3 sts, skip next 2 sts, dc in each of next 3 sts; rep from * around, ending with skip 2 sts, join in top of beg ch-3.

Rnd 9: Sl st in next st, ch 3, dc in each of next 3 sts, *Shell in ch-2 sp, dc in each of next 4 sts, skip next 2 sts, dc in each of next 4 sts; rep from * around, ending with skip next 2 sts, join in top of beg ch-3. Continue in this manner, working pattern as set in Rnds 7, 8 and 9 (having 2 more dc on each rep between shells, except Rnd 7 which uses the Small Shell), working in color sequence as follows:

Please Note: It is important to work the Small Shell on Rnd 7 to keep the afghan smooth and not to run out of yarn.

Rnds 10 and 11: Use 2 strands Color 5.

Rnds 12 and 13: Use one strand Color 5, one strand Color 4.

Rnds 14 and 15: Use 2 strands Color 4.

Rnds 16 and 17: Use one strand Color 4 and one strand Color 3.

Rnds 18 and 19: Use 2 strands Color 3.

Rnds 20 and 21: Use one strand Color 3 and one strand Color 2.

Rnds 22 and 23: Use 2 stands Color 2.

Rnds 24 and 25: Use one strand Color 2 and one strand Color 1.

Rnds 26 and 27: Use 2 strands Color 1.

Break yarn and fasten off.

Sew in all ends.

Baby Diagonal Blanket

 INTERMEDIATE

SHOPPING LIST

Yarn (Worsted Weight) MEDIUM 4

[6 ounces, 315 yards
(170 grams, 288 meters) per skein]:

- ☐ Color A White - 2 skeins
- ☐ Color B Lilac - 1 skein
- ☐ Color C Blue - 1 skein
- ☐ Color D Aqua - 1 skein
- ☐ Color E Pink - 1 skein
- ☐ Color F Yellow - 1 skein

Crochet Hook

- ☐ Size 7 (4.50 mm)
  or size needed for gauge

SIZE INFORMATION

Size: 32 x 40" (81.5 x 101.5 cm)

GAUGE INFORMATION

4 Blocks (each Block is ch 3, 3 dc) to 3" [7.5 cm], using suggested hook or any size hook which will give the correct gauge.

—— STITCH GUIDE ——

Note: This blanket is worked in diagonal stripes, beginning at the lower right corner and ending at the upper left corner.

Also, when pattern says to turn (following ch 6), do this by flipping the previous block or blocks so that the turning ch-spaces are always at the top of the work.

_____

INSTRUCTIONS

Starting at lower right corner.

Row 1: Using Color A, ch 6, *dc in 4th ch from hook (3 skipped chs count as turning ch-sp), and each of next 2 ch* - **Beg Block made**. Row 1 is complete.

Row 2: Ch 6, turn (flip previous block so the turning ch-sp is at top of work), dc in 4th ch from hook and each of next 2 ch - Beg Block of 2nd Row made.
Hold previous Block close to last block made, and sl st in turning ch-sp (which is at top of block), ch 3, 3 dc in same sp - **Block made**. Row 2 is complete.

Row 3: Ch 6, turn as before, work a Beg Block as in Row 1, then work 2 Blocks. Row 3 is complete.

Row 4: Ch 6, turn as before, work a Beg Block, work 3 Blocks. Row 4 is complete. Finish off Color A.

Row 5: Join Color B with a sl st in last dc made, ch 6, turn as before, work a Beg Block, work 4 Blocks. Row 5 is complete.

Continue in this manner, having one more Block per row. Do not carry colors not in use.

Break yarn and finish off each time colors are changed.

Now work in the following color sequence:

Rows 6-7: Use Color B.

Row 8: Use Color A.

Rows 9-11: Use Color B.

Rows 12-15: Use Color A.

Rows 16-18: Use Color C.

Row 19: Use Color A.

Rows 20-22: Use Color C.

Rows 23-26: Use Color A.

Rows 27-29: Use Color D.

Row 30: Use Color A.

Rows 31-33: Use Color D.

Rows 34-37: Use Color A.

Rows 38-40: Use Color E.

Row 41: Use Color A.

Row 42: (lower left corner) Do Not work a Beg Block, turn as before and join Color E with a sl st in ch-3 space of last block made in Row 41, ch 3, 3 dc in same space, complete row as before.

Row 43: Ch 6, turn, work a Beg Block, complete row as before.

Row 44: Turn, sl st in each of next 3 dc and into ch-3 space, ch 3, work 3 dc in same space, complete row as before.

Rows 45-48: Using Color A, work Beg Blocks on Rows 45 and 47, but not on Rows 46 and 48.

Rows 49-51: Using Color F, work Beg Blocks on Rows 49 and 51, but not on Row 50.

Row 52: (upper right corner) Using Color A, work as Row 44.

Row 53: Using Color F, turn and join with a sl st in ch-3 space of last block made in Row 52, ch 3, 3 dc in same space, complete row as before.

Now continue in the following color sequences, starting each row with "sl st to ch-3 sp" or "join new color with sl st in ch-3 sp..."; there are no more Beg Blocks worked, and each row will have one less block than previous row:

Rows 54 and 55: Use Color F.

Rows 56-59: Use Color A.

Rows 60-62: Use Color D.

Row 63: Use Color A.

Rows 64-66: Use Color D.

Rows 67-70: Use Color A.

Rows 71-73: Use Color C.

Row 74: Use Color A.

Rows 75-77: Use Color C.

Rows 78-81: Use Color A.

Rows 82-84: Use Color B.

Row 85: Use Color A.

Rows 86-88: Use Color B.

Rows 89-92: Use Color A.

Break yarn and fasten off. Weave in all ends.

Border: With right side of blanket facing, join Color F with a sl st in upper right corner.

Rnd 1: Sc in same space, work 7 dc in space between 1st and 2nd Blocks, sc in space between 2nd and 3rd Blocks, *7 dc in next space between Blocks, sc in next space between Blocks; rep from * around afghan, join with sl st in first sc. Break yarn and fasten off.

ASSEMBLY DIAGRAM

	turning ch-sp		
Row 4 Block 1			
Row 3 Block 3	Row 4 Block 2	turning ch-sp	
Row 2 Block 1	Row 3 Block 2	Row 4 Block 3	turning ch-sp
Row 1 Block 1	Row 2 Block 2	Row 3 Block 1	Row 4 Block 4 / turning ch-sp

General Instructions

ABBREVIATIONS

"	inches
approx.	approximately
beg	begin or beginning
CC	Contrast Color
ch	chain
cm	centimeters
dc	double crochet
dec	decrease or decreasing
gm	gram
hdc	half double crochet
inc	increase or increasing
MC	Main Color
mm	millimeter
rem	remain or remaining
rep	repeat
rnd(s)	round(s)
sc	single crochet
sl	slip
sp(s)	spaces(s)
st(s)	stitch(es)
tog	together
tr	treble crochet
trc	triple crochet
yds	yards
yo	yarn over hook

* or # work instructions following or between * or # as many more times as indicated in addition to the first time.

() or [ ] work enclosed instructions as many times as specified by the number immediately following or work all enclosed instructions in the stitch or space indicated or contains explanatory remarks

— the number(s) given after a hyphen at the end of a row or round denote(s) the number of stitches or spaces you should have on that row or round.

■□□□□ BEGINNER	Projects for first-time crocheters using basic stitches. Minimal shaping.
■■□□□ EASY	Projects using yarn with basic stitches, repetitive stitch patterns, simple color changes, and simple shaping and finishing.
■■■□□ INTERMEDIATE	Projects using a variety of techniques, such as basic lace patterns or color patterns, mid-level shaping and finishing.
■■■■□ EXPERIENCED	Projects with intricate stitch patterns, techniques and dimension, such as non-repeating patterns, multi-color techniques, fine threads, small hooks, detailed shaping and refined finishing.

Yarn Weight Symbol & Names	1 SUPER FINE	2 FINE	3 LIGHT	4 MEDIUM	5 BULKY	6 SUPER BULKY
Type of Yarns in Category	Sock, Fingering Baby	Sport, Baby	DK, Light Worsted	Worsted, Afghan Aran	Chunky, Craft, Rug	Bulky, Roving
Crochet Gauge* Ranges in Single Crochet to 4" (10 cm)	21-32 sts	16-20 sts	12-17 sts	11-14 sts	8-11 sts	5-9 sts
Advised Hook Size Range	B-1 to E-4	E-4 to 7	7 to I-9	I-9 to K-10.5	K-10.5 to M-13	M-13 and larger

*GUIDELINES ONLY: The chart above reflects the most commonly used gauges and hook sizes for specific yarn categories.

CROCHET HOOKS												
Metric mm	2.25	2.75	3.25	3.5	3.75	4	5	5.5	6	6.5	9	10	15
U.S.	B-1	C-2	D-3	E-4	F-5	G-6	H-8	I-9	J-10	K-10.5	N	P	Q

CROCHET TERMINOLOGY		
UNITED STATES		INTERNATIONAL
slip stitch (slip st)	=	single crochet (sc)
single crochet (sc)	=	double crochet (dc)
half double crochet (hdc)	=	half treble crochet (htr)
double crochet (dc)	=	treble crochet (tr)
treble crochet (tr)	=	double treble crochet (dtr)
double treble crochet (dtr)	=	triple treble crochet (ttr)
triple treble crochet (ttr)	=	quadruple treble crochet (qtr)
skip	=	miss

Slip Knot

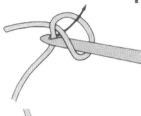

1. Make a loop, then hook another loop through it.

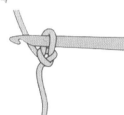

2. Tighten gently and slide the knot up to the hook.

Chain Stitch (ch)

1. Yarn over hook (yo) and draw the yarn through to form a new loop without tightening up the previous one.

2. Repeat to form as many chains (ch) as required. Do not count the slip knot as a stitch.

Slip Stitch (sl st)

This is the shortest crochet stitch and unlike other stitches is not used on its own to produce a fabric. It is used for joining, shaping and where necessary carrying the yarn to another part of the fabric for the next stage.

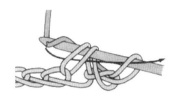

Insert hook into work (second chain from hook), yarn over hook (yo) and draw the yarn through both the work and loop on hook in one movement.

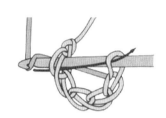

To join a chain ring with a slip stitch (sl st), insert hook into first chain (ch), yarn over hook (yo) and draw through both the work and the yarn on hook in one movement.

Single Crochet (sc)

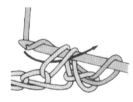

1. Insert the hook into the work (2nd chain (ch) from hook on starting chain), yarn over hook (yo) and draw yarn through the work only.

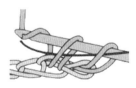

2. Yarn over hook (yo) again and draw the yarn through both loops on the hook.

3. 1 single crochet (sc) made. Insert hook into next stitch: repeat (rep) from * in step 1.

Half Double Crochet (hdc)

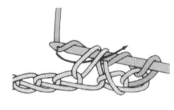

1. Yarn over hook (yo) and insert the hook into the work (3rd chain (ch) from hook on starting chain) and draw through the work only.

2. Yarn over hook (yo) again and draw through all three loops on the hook.

3. 1 hdc made. Yarn over hook (yo), insert hook into next stitch (st), repeat (rep) from step 2.

Double Crochet (dc)

1. Yarn over hook (yo) and insert the hook into the work (4th chain from hook on starting chain) and draw through the work only.

3. Yarn over hook (yo) and draw through the last two loops on the hook.

2. Yarn over hook (yo) and draw through the first two loops only.

4. 1 dc made. Yarn over hook (yo), insert hook into next stitch (st); repeat (rep) from step 2.

Yarn Information

Projects in this book were made with sportweight or medium weight yarns. Any brand of yarn may be used. It is best to refer to yardage/meters when determining how many balls or skeins to purchase. Remember, to arrive at the finished size, it is the GAUGE/TENSION that is important, not the brand of yarn. For your convenience, listed below are the specific yarn ranges used to create our photographed models.

Sugar Spun Blanket
Mary Maxim's® Sugar Baby Stripes

Baby Diamonds Blanket
Mary Maxim's® Baby's Best

Bears on My Blanket
Mary Maxim's® Baby's Best
Mary Maxim's® Ultra Mellowspun

Tiny Bubbles Blanket
Caron® Simply Soft®

Duckies Blanket
Mary Maxim's® Starlette

Peaceful Pastels Afghan
Bernat® Baby Coordinates

Baby Diagonal Blanket
Mary Maxim's® Baby Value